CW01082940

Original title:
Visionary Thinking

Author: Paul Pääsuke
ISBN HARDBACK: 978-9916-87-026-6
ISBN PAPERBACK: 978-9916-87-027-3

Ethereal Clarity

In the silence of the night,
Stars whisper dreams awake,
A clarity ethereal,
In the stillness, we take.

Reflections dance like shadows,
In the pools of the mind,
Guiding thoughts like rivers,
To what's gentle and kind.

Breathe in the soft moments,
Let the chaos lay still,
In the heart's gentle echo,
Find the peace you will.

Each whisper is a promise,
In the depths of the soul,
With clarity ethereal,
Become beautifully whole.

So seek the light within you,
Let it shimmer and glow,
In ethereal clarity,
Let your true self show.

Whispers of the Unwritten

Pages turn like seasons,
Unwritten tales await,
In the quiet of the evening,
Starts a fateful date.

With every breath, potential,
Stories long to be told,
Whispers of the unwritten,
Turn to brave and bold.

Ink flows with ambitions,
As dreams begin to rise,
Fleeting thoughts like feathers,
Embrace the endless skies.

In the heartbeats of moments,
The unwritten calls us near,
To chase the hidden pathways,
And face away our fear.

So weave the threads of passion,
And let your spirit flow,
In whispers of the unwritten,
Find the magic to grow.

Blueprint of the Mind's Eye

Sketches drawn in a silent space,
Imagination breathes with grace.
Colors blend in abstract forms,
In the mind where the spirit warms.

Lines converge, a vision grows,
Through twisted paths, the wanderer goes.
Each thought a stroke upon the page,
Creating art that cannot age.

Echoes of the Unforeseen

In shadows dance the echoes,
Whispers of what lies ahead,
Each footstep leaves a story,
A path where dreams have fled.

Through mist upon the mountains,
The future softly calls,
Guiding hearts through silence,
Breaking haunting walls.

Moments lost in twilight,
Time drifts like a stream,
The unseen beckons gently,
Unraveling the dream.

With every breath of darkness,
A light begins to bloom,
Hope intertwines with sorrow,
In the silence, there's room.

So listen to the echoes,
Let them guide your way,
For in the unforeseen whispers,
A new dawn greets the day.

The Canvas of Change

Brushstrokes of the morning,
Colors bright and bold,
Each hue a new beginning,
As stories unfold.

The winds of time are blowing,
Shaping all we see,
Transforming our tomorrow,
With each vivid plea.

Moments blend and mingle,
On this canvas vast,
With shadows and with light,
Creating futures cast.

Every heart an artist,
Every soul a part,
Together we create it,
A masterpiece of art.

So take the brush, dear dreamer,
And paint with strength your truth,
For in this realm of change,
Lies the wisdom of youth.

Gates to New Dimensions

Through twilight's veil, a door unfolds,
Whispered dreams in colors bold.
A tapestry of paths anew,
Inviting souls to journey through.

Each step taken in curious light,
Hidden realms come into sight.
Echoes of the ancients call,
In these chambers, we find it all.

Time dances on a cosmic thread,
Woven stories of those long dead.
In the silence, secrets bloom,
As we wander, we find our room.

Beyond the veil, the stars align,
Fates entwined in space and time.
Gates swing wide, we dare to roam,
In this vastness, we find our home.

With hearts aglow, we cross the line,
Into dimensions, so divine.
The journey's end, just a start,
In every corner, there beats a heart.

The Cartographer of Aspirations

With ink and dreams, the map is drawn,
Each wish a star, each hope a dawn.
Landscapes crafted in the mind,
Trails of passion intertwine.

Where the mountains rise with pride,
And rivers of purpose swiftly glide.
Through valleys deep and skies so wide,
The cartographer's heart, the ultimate guide.

In every line, a story told,
Of brave pursuits and dreams of gold.
With every stroke, the future calls,
Boundless potential behind the walls.

This canvas vast, yet intricately small,
Holds the weight of aspirations for all.
A journey waiting, just set free,
To chart the course of destiny.

Let the compass point to the true,
With every heartbeat, seek what's due.
For in each map, a chance to grow,
A path laid out, for brave souls to go.

The Architects of Thought

In silence they construct their dreams,
With hammers made of ideas and beams.
Each twist of fate, a brick laid true,
Minds entwined, creating something new.

Blueprints whispered in the night,
Plans unfurling, hearts take flight.
Visionaries sketching worlds so wide,
In the realm where thoughts abide.

The Forge of New Ideas

In the fire, imagination's heat,
Where thoughts alone, dare to meet.
From ashes rise, concepts ignite,
In the forge, dreams take flight.

With hammer strikes, shape and mold,
Ideas crafted, brave and bold.
Anvil's song, a rhythmic beat,
Creating wonders, oh so sweet.

Through sparks that dance in twilight's glow,
Wisdom flows, like rivers slow.
In this sanctuary, visions form,
A cradle for the mind's great storm.

Collaboration fuels the flame,
Voices rise, none feel the shame.
In unity, our purpose clear,
Constructing futures, year by year.

At last, the creations shine anew,
Each piece a story that's born of you.
The forge awaits with open door,
Inviting all to dream and soar.

Spinning the Web of Tomorrow

Threads of silver, woven tight,
In the loom of endless night.
Future whispers, softly spun,
A tapestry 'neath the rising sun.

Patterns dance in gentle sway,
Shaping dreams for a brand new day.
Each strand a hope, each knot a wish,
As visions merge in a vibrant dish.

Weaving tales yet to be told,
In colors vivid, strong, and bold.
A network rich, connections grow,
As we dare to dream, to flow.

With every spin, our stories share,
In the fabric, we find our care.
Together we craft, together we write,
The web of tomorrow, pure and bright.

So let us gather, hearts entwined,
In this design, our fate aligned.
Through the web, we reach and find,
A world reborn, forever kind.

The Architecture of Aspirations

In the quiet dawn of dreams,
Foundations lay in whispered schemes.
Brick by brick, courage builds high,
Reaching upwards, as hopes fly.

Walls adorned with visions bright,
Windows open to the light.
Each corner carved with intent clear,
A structure bold, made without fear.

A roof that shelters every wish,
Embracing passions as they swish.
Staircases lead to what we seek,
Elevating spirits that feel weak.

Rooms filled with laughter and grace,
Echoes of joy, a warm embrace.
Each door opens, inviting chance,
An architecture born from dance.

So lay the plans, sketch the dreams,
In every heart, potential gleams.
Construct a life where hopes reside,
In the architecture, let love guide.

Gazing into the Crystal Future

Shimmering light bends through the glass,
Reflections show the days that pass.
A tapestry woven with hopes and fears,
Embracing all our laughter and tears.

Stars align in a dance of fate,
Possibilities open a tempting gate.
With every glance, a path to take,
In the stillness, dreams awake.

Lighthouse of Future Visions

Standing tall against the night,
A beacon casting ancient light.
Guiding ships on restless seas,
Hope ignited in the breeze.

Waves crash with stories untold,
Dreams ahead, fierce and bold.
With every pulse, the light will shine,
A lighthouse bright, forever divine.

The lantern glows, a steady beam,
Illuminating a distant dream.
Through storms and clouds, it will hold true,
A guardian watchful, ever new.

Night may fall, shadows will creep,
Yet in its glow, the lost will leap.
Across the water, visions gleam,
In the lighthouse, we find our dream.

So let your heart be the ship that sails,
Navigating through life's gales.
With the lighthouse lighting each way,
Future visions guide our stay.

Fragments of an Unwritten Odyssey

In pages blank, the journey starts,
With ink and dreams, we play our parts.
Each line a step, a tale to weave,
In fragments, we learn to believe.

Mountains rise in silent thought,
Each peak a lesson, dearly sought.
The valleys hold the shadows cast,
In written echoes of the past.

Waves of doubt may crash and break,
Yet within us, we still awake.
Through every storm, each raindrop's song,
In fragments, we learn to be strong.

The stars align to guide our way,
In the dark, they softly sway.
The odyssey waits, both wild and free,
In unwritten dreams, we find what's we.

Embrace the journey, take each stride,
In fragments, let your spirit guide.
Craft your tale with heart and pen,
An odyssey awaits you, again and again.

Blueprints of Belief

Drawn in lines of hope and trust,
Blueprints made from faith's own dust.
Each stroke a testament of grace,
In every heart, belief finds place.

Pillars rise from whispered dreams,
Supporting all that hope redeems.
With colors bright, the plans unfold,
A symphony of stories told.

In every margin, visions flare,
Guiding hands, and minds that dare.
Through trials faced, a courage found,
Blueprints of belief, forever sound.

Let faith be certain, strong and bold,
Beyond the canvas, stories unfold.
In schemes and dreams, we pave the way,
With blueprints drawn, we seize the day.

So sketch the paths of what's to come,
In every heartbeat, find the drum.
Through belief, the world takes flight,
And in its glow, we find our light.

Beyond the Expected

In shadows cast by time's embrace,
We find the light that leaves a trace.
Beyond the walls of what we know,
A world unfolds, begins to glow.

The winds of change whisper softly,
Suggesting paths that yearn to be.
Each step we take, a daring leap,
Into the realms where secrets seep.

With hearts unbound and spirits free,
We challenge fate's own decree.
Courage blooms in every dream,
As we unravel life's great scheme.

In every twist, a chance to grow,
In every turn, a chance to know.
Beyond the expected we shall soar,
Awakening to evermore.

Embrace the unknown, dance with fate,
In the spaces where hope awaits.
Beyond the expected, we shall find,
The beauty crafted by the mind.

The Path Less Taken

Amidst the woods where silence hums,
A trail emerges, soft and numb.
With each step along this route,
The whispers beckon, dreams pursue.

The world outside may seem so bright,
But here lies magic, pure delight.
A path less traveled, wild and free,
A journey forged in mystery.

Beneath the leaves where shadows play,
A secret song calls us to stay.
In nature's arms, where time is still,
We carve our way with strength and will.

Each winding turn, a story found,
In every moment, life unbound.
The path less taken, rich and wise,
Leads to horizons, endless skies.

So let us wander, hand in hand,
Through uncharted fields, wandering land.
For in this space, our hearts awaken,
To the gift of the path less taken.

Navigating Uncharted Dreams

Sailing seas of the unknown,
With stars as guides, we venture alone.
Mapping routes through the darkened skies,
Exploring realms where the heart complies.

Winds may shift, waves may rise,
Yet courage sparks in restless sighs.
With every turn, a chance to glean,
New horizons in visions unseen.

Insights Hidden in Time

Through layers deep of yesterdays,
Wisdom glimmers in gentle rays.
Insights hidden, softly speak,
In quiet corners, shadows peek.

The clock ticks on with steadfast might,
Yet echoes linger, soft and bright.
Memories forge the paths we tread,
Each moment cherished, never dead.

In history's book, we find our guide,
Each page a spark where dreams abide.
The lessons learned, though often blurred,
In time's embrace, their voice is heard.

As seasons change and ages flow,
The past holds answers we should know.
Deep in the silence, truths unwind,
Insights hidden, for heart and mind.

Let us seek comfort, seek the light,
In the mysteries of day and night.
With open hearts, we shall ascend,
To the whispers time loves to send.

Labyrinths of the Future

In mazes formed by dreams untold,
The future dances, bright and bold.
Each twist and turn, a choice to make,
A woven path, a journey's wake.

Stars above, our guiding light,
Through shadows cast and endless night.
In labyrinths, we learn to see,
The endless possibilities to be.

With courage as our steady flame,
We face the doubt, we stake our claim.
The future calls, a siren's song,
In its embrace, we can belong.

So follow closely, step by step,
In every breath, remember, prep.
For in the labyrinth, wisdom waits,
To show us dreams that love creates.

Let visions spark, let hearts ignite,
In labyrinths where hope takes flight.
The future's promise, wild and true,
Awaits the brave, the bold—like you.

The Art of Knowing More

With each question asked, new doors appear,
The quest for knowledge, ever so dear.
Whispers of wisdom in silence grow,
In every heartbeat, a chance to know.

In shadows of doubt, light starts to creep,
The layers of truth, in layers we sweep.
To learn is to dance with the thoughts that flow,
A beauty in seeking what lies below.

A Dance with Destiny

In twilight's glow we sway,
Our paths entwined in fate,
The stars above us play,
As dreams we co-create.

Each step a whispered chance,
In rhythm, hearts align,
With every daring glance,
We trace the grand design.

The winds of change do call,
Guiding us through the night,
Together we will fall,
And rise in shared delight.

With laughter as our guide,
We twirl in endless space,
No fear as we confide,
In this sweet, daring chase.

So take my hand, let's soar,
Beyond the fields of dreams,
A dance forevermore,
In life's unfolding themes.

Cultivating Tomorrow's Seeds

With tender hands we dig,
In soil of hope and grace,
We plant each tiny sprig,
And nurture dreams in place.

The sunlight kisses ground,
As rains of fortune fall,
In silence, life is found,
Through nature's wondrous call.

Each seed a world in wait,
To blossom, grow, and shine,
With patience, we await,
The fruits of love divine.

Through toil, our spirits lift,
In gardens rich and rare,
Each moment is a gift,
A promise in the air.

So let's cultivate the dreams,
And watch as they take flight,
In unity it seems,
We shape our shared delight.

The Imagineer's Odyssey

Beneath the stars I wander,
In realms of endless dreams,
Where visions pull me fonder,
And light spills through moonbeams.

With colors bright and bold,
I sketch the world anew,
With stories yet untold,
And paths that I pursue.

Through forests made of glass,
And mountains drawn with thread,
I seek each moment's pass,
Where whispers dare to tread.

In every thought, a spark,
A map to venture far,
Through shadows, light, and dark,
I'll follow every star.

So let the journey start,
With courage in my heart,
In this grand tapestry,
I'll weave my destiny.

Serendipity in Thought

A chance glance on the street,
Where eyes and smiles collide,
A moment bittersweet,
In fate, we learn to bide.

With gentle hands of fate,
We weave the threads we find,
In small things, oh so great,
A serendipitous bind.

Like whispers in the breeze,
Instincts softly speak,
In laughter, hearts at ease,
To strangers, we're not weak.

A fleeting touch, a sigh,
A note that floats along,
In silence, questions lie,
Yet somehow, we are strong.

So cherish every chance,
Embrace the paths we walk,
In life's sweet, waltzing dance,
We find our hearts in talk.

Bridge to the Infinite

Across the river of dreams, they flow,
Whispers of stars in the night glow.
Step by step, the journey unfolds,
Each heartbeat a story, each moment holds.

Beneath the arch of time's embrace,
We wander through shadows, seeking grace.
Hands reach for more, for the unknown,
In the vastness, we find our own.

With every bridge that we dare to cross,
We learn of gains, we learn of loss.
In the silence, truths softly gleam,
A dance of hope, a fragile dream.

Through stormy skies, the colors blend,
Where each beginning meets its end.
Journey on, brave hearts of light,
For in the end, we take flight.

So let the stars be your guide,
Across the chasm, side by side.
Onward we march, in unity's thrall,
Together we rise, together we fall.

Awakening the Infinite

In the hush of dawn, a spark ignites,
Endless skies call forth soft, warm lights.
Mountains stand guard, timeless and wise,
Nature unfolds, where the spirit flies.

Waves of the ocean kiss the shore,
A dance of possibilities, forever more.
In the heart of stillness, truth is found,
Awakening the soul, profound and sound.

Paintbrush of Possibility

With every stroke, a world is born,
Colors dance, where dreams are worn.
A canvas blank, yet full of grace,
Infinite paths in time and space.

Bright hues of hope mix with despair,
A swirl of joy, in the vibrant air.
Each splash a choice, a chance to create,
Life's masterpiece, we now narrate.

From shadows dark, to sunlight's kiss,
We sketch the moments, both pain and bliss.
In every corner, stories reside,
As the heart takes wings, and learns to glide.

Across the palette, futures collide,
In the hands of dreamers, visions abide.
Paintbrush held firm, we're never alone,
In the gallery of life, truth is shown.

Brush on, dear spirit, let colors run free,
In the world of possibility.
For each stroke you make lays the foundation,
Of a vibrant, unique creation.

Echoes of Imagined Futures

In whispered winds, the futures hide,
A tapestry woven, where hopes abide.
Through portals of thought, we dare to dream,
In the echoes, reality may gleam.

Time travelers of the heart and mind,
We paint in silence, contours unlined.
Each echo whispers of paths we seek,
A promise of change in the stillness peak.

Beneath the stars, our visions converge,
In the glowing twilight, creation's surge.
With each heartbeat, we shape the day,
In the murmurs of night, new worlds sway.

What lies ahead in the realms unseen?
Possibilities breathe where dreams have been.
Awaken the echoes, let them ignite,
In the chorus of dawn, we find our light.

So listen closely, let visions unfurl,
Each thought a ripple in time's great whirl.
For the future calls, a beckoning tune,
In the heart of the night, beneath the moon.

The Chisel of Change

With every strike, we carve our fate,
A sculptor's hands mold what we create.
Chiseling through the stone of fear,
Emerging forms that sparkle near.

Old patterns break, like chains undone,
In the dance of life, we find the sun.
Each chip reveals a deeper truth,
In the creation of eternal youth.

The granite hard, yet soft within,
Where shadows linger, new lights begin.
With each decision, we shape our space,
In the gallery of time, we find our place.

Trust the process, let the hammer ring,
Through trials faced, the spirit takes wing.
A masterpiece waits in the dust and clay,
With the chisel of change, we mold our way.

So wield it gently, this tool of hope,
In every crack, we learn to cope.
For in the changes, our beauty lies,
Awakening visions beneath the skies.

The Light of Unexplored Pathways

In the woods where shadows dwell,
Silent whispers softly tell.
Footsteps echo, softly tread,
Chasing dreams where few have led.

Lanterns flicker, guiding sight,
Through the dark, a thread of light.
Faint but sure, they lead us on,
Towards the break of early dawn.

Twists and turns along the way,
Mysteries in disarray.
Each rustle speaks of paths anew,
In the quiet, hope imbues.

Nature dances, shadows play,
In the light of each new day.
With open hearts, we walk the road,
Together lifting every load.

Step by step, the journey flows,
Through the meadows, where magic grows.
In unseen realms, our spirits soar,
The unexplored calls for more.

Dreamscapes of Tomorrow

In the twilight, dreams take flight,
Painting visions, bold and bright.
Through the clouds, we drift and sway,
In this land where we can play.

Future whispers, soft and clear,
Voices beckon us to hear.
Woven threads of hopes and fears,
In this dreamscape, time disappears.

Stars above, they shine and gleam,
Guiding us through every dream.
With each thought, a world does spin,
For in dreaming, we begin.

Across horizons made of light,
Every heart ignites the night.
Boundless joy, untamed and free,
Together shaping destiny.

Tomorrow waits with open arms,
Awaiting us with all its charms.
In this space, we claim our place,
In dreamscapes, full of grace.

The Horizon's Whisper

Beyond the hills, where sun dips low,
A whisper rides the evening glow.
Secrets linger in the breeze,
Carried softly through the trees.

Golden rays kiss the land,
Painting shadows with a hand.
Promises wrapped in twilight haze,
A gentle end to bustling days.

Each breath a tale, each sigh a song,
Carving paths where we belong.
As night unfolds with stars in sight,
The horizon calls, a new delight.

In stillness, dreams begin to bloom,
Illuminating every room.
With open hearts, we seek and find,
The quiet echoes of the mind.

With every dawn, the journey grows,
The horizon's whisper, the heart knows.
Into the depths of time we glide,
Onward, where dreams coincide.

Eyes Beyond the Stars

Through the vastness, wonders gleam,
In the night, we chase a dream.
Stars above, a dance of light,
Guiding souls through endless night.

With eyes wide, we gaze afar,
Searching for our guiding star.
Each twinkle holds a story deep,
In silence, the cosmos speaks.

Voices echo in the night,
Whispers of a distant flight.
We yearn to touch the great unknown,
Where stardust seeds are gently sown.

Every heartbeat, every sigh,
Draws us closer to the sky.
In our dreams, we soar and rise,
With eyes wide open to the skies.

As constellations twine and weave,
In their glow, we choose to believe.
In a universe of endless charms,
We find our place in celestial arms.

The Alchemy of Ideas

Thoughts like gold dust shimmer bright,
They dance and twist in the soft night.
In dreams we mold, with hearts ablaze,
We craft our visions in a daze.

Whispers of brilliance, soft yet loud,
Transforming silence into a crowd.
Each notion sparks a fiery glow,
Building bridges where none did grow.

From chaos springs a wondrous shape,
A tapestry that will escape.
With hands of kin, we forge anew,
A legacy that feels so true.

In every heartbeat, wisdom flows,
A river deep where knowledge grows.
The alchemist's hand can shape the clay,
Turning moments into the day.

So let us gather, let us share,
These fragments, bursting with flair.
For in our hearts, the magic lies,
The alchemy of our own skies.

Mosaics of Tomorrow

Pieces scattered on the ground,
Each one a story, echoing sound.
Together they dance, they sing in glee,
Forming the future, wild and free.

Colors bright as the sun's embrace,
Infusing passion with gentle grace.
Every shard, a vision anew,
A glimpse of the life we'll weave through.

We gather fragments of hopes and dreams,
Carving a path in radiant beams.
With each connection, we understand,
Together we rise, as a band.

In shadows cast by yesterday's light,
We piece together what feels so right.
Crafting a world where all belong,
In unity's heart, we grow strong.

So let us cherish, let us compose,
These mosaics, where love overflows.
In shared visions, we find our way,
Mending the dawn of a new day.

Awakened Imagination

In slumber's realm, where dreams take flight,
Imagination stirs in the night.
A canvas blank, ready to be,
Awakening visions, wild and free.

We venture forth, minds unconfined,
Chasing the wonders we long to find.
With heartbeats racing, we explore,
The realms of magic, forevermore.

Each thought a spark igniting the dark,
Painting the skies with vivid mark.
Unbound by limits, we dare to roam,
Creating a world we can call home.

In whispers soft, inspiration flows,
An endless river that gently grows.
Through every heartbeat, we start anew,
A journey of colors, bright and true.

So let us dream, let fantasies soar,
In the tapestry of life, we restore.
Awakened imagination leads the way,
Filling our lives with endless play.

Shadows of What Lies Ahead

In twilight's hush, the shadows grow,
Whispers of what we cannot know.
Paths untraveled, drawn in light,
Carving visions just out of sight.

With every step, the future unfolds,
Stories hidden, yet to be told.
In uncertainty, we find our grace,
Facing the shadows that we must embrace.

Echoes linger from the past,
Guiding our feet, so bold and vast.
Each moment shapes what's yet to come,
Resonating like a distant drum.

In layers deep, our hopes reside,
Fighting against the rising tide.
With courage bright, we face our fears,
Transforming doubt into heartfelt cheers.

So let us wander, let us seek,
In the shadows, the brave grow sleek.
For what lies ahead is ours to mold,
In the canvas of life, dreams unfold.

The Craft of the Dreamer

In twilight's glow the dreamers meet,
They weave their visions, bold and sweet.
With whispered hopes and starlit eyes,
They paint the darkened, silent skies.

Through shadows deep, their stories flow,
On canvas bright, their spirits grow.
A spark ignites with every breath,
In dreams, they dance beyond the death.

From ashes rise the crafted fate,
As night unfolds, they contemplate.
Each thread they pull brings forth the light,
The tapestry of endless night.

With every heartbeat, dreams take flight,
Through realms unknown, they chase the light.
A journey carved in cosmic dust,
In dreams, they find their fervent trust.

The world awakens to their art,
As dreamers play their vital part.
In unity, they shape the day,
The craft of dreams will find its way.

Seeds of Change

In quiet soil, the seeds are sown,
A whisper stirs, a life is grown.
With patient hands, the earth bestows,
The hope that every moment knows.

Beneath the sun, the roots entwine,
In silent trust, the stars align.
The gentle rain will wash the ground,
In every drop, new life is found.

Each bud unfurls with colors bright,
A testament to endless fight.
Through seasons' grasp, they stretch and bend,
The seeds of change will never end.

They break the surface, reach for air,
In every heart, a vital care.
With every bloom, the world awakes,
A symphony that nature makes.

Through storms that rage, they stand their ground,
Resilient hope in every sound.
With roots in dreams, they find their way,
The seeds of change will always stay.

Clouds of Infinite Thought

In skies of blue, the clouds compose,
A canvas vast where thought bestows.
With whispers soft, they start to form,
Ideas swirl in every storm.

Each shape that shifts, a mind set free,
In fleeting dreams, they come to be.
Through gusts of wind, they intertwine,
The dance of thought, a grand design.

Floating high, they challenge norms,
Evolving shapes through endless storms.
In fleeting views, a truth revealed,
As insights bloom, their fate is sealed.

From wispy hints to thunderous roars,
A journey mapped on boundless shores.
The clouds above, a world of lore,
In every thought, a whispered score.

They scatter light, they bend and twist,
In realms of thought, we coexist.
With every drift, new dreams ignite,
The clouds of thought take sudden flight.

Realms of Possibility

Beyond the veil, where shadows play,
Lie realms of hope, a bright array.
In every step, a choice is made,
To forge the path, the plans displayed.

With open hearts, we seek the way,
In whispered dreams, the signs will sway.
Each turn we take sparks new designs,
In endless fields, our fate aligns.

The maps we draw, with colors bold,
Tell stories waiting to be told.
With courage found in every breath,
We dance the line 'twixt life and death.

Beyond the stars, a world awaits,
In silent hopes, we find our fates.
The doors we knock, the paths we take,
In realms of dreams, the rules will break.

With every heartbeat, life unfolds,
A tapestry of dreams retold.
Together we will weave the light,
In realms of possibility, we fight.

Uncharted Terrains of Thought

In the quiet depths we ponder,
Paths untread call out like thunder.
Ideas bloom where shadows fall,
In the stillness, we hear their call.

Maps are drawn with fleeting ink,
To places where we cease to think.
Thoughts like rivers, twist and bend,
In the maze, we seek to mend.

Through the fog, a light sparkles,
Whispers echo, soft and starkles.
Each moment unfolds its face,
In this boundless, sacred space.

We delve deeper, unafraid,
In the mind's vast serenade.
Braving storms, we find our way,
Through the night, towards the day.

Together, we sail the unknown,
On waves of thought, seeds are sown.
As horizons invite our gaze,
We journey on through life's maze.

The Pulse of Uncreated Dreams

In the silence, dreams awaken,
Threads of magic, softly shaken.
Each heartbeat a whispering spark,
Igniting the flame in the dark.

Visions swirl in cosmic dance,
A symphony of wild romance.
Questions linger in the air,
As possibilities lay bare.

Fractals of hope paint the night,
Colors blend, creating light.
In this realm where thoughts unite,
We carve our wishes, taking flight.

Breath of wonder fills the void,
Each moment cherished, not destroyed.
Time slips by like grains of sand,
In the rhythm, we make our stand.

In endless skies, we cast our nets,
Hoping to catch dreams without regrets.
Tangled vines of fate entwine,
In the pulse of dreams divine.

Patterns in the Cosmic Canvas

Stars are brushed with strokes of fate,
Each one holding tales innate.
In the dark, they twist and weave,
Guiding hearts that dare believe.

Galaxies swirl in endless grace,
Infinite forms in boundless space.
Constellations whisper tales,
Of journeys vast on cosmic trails.

Colors merge in twilight's glow,
Mysteries birthed, unknown to show.
Each moment a brush against time,
Creating rhythms, a silent rhyme.

With open eyes, we start to see,
How every dot connects to be.
In chaos, beauty finds its sway,
Painting dreams in shades of gray.

Let us wander, souls set free,
In the patterns of the cosmic sea.
For within each thread and seam,
Lies the essence of a dream.

Embracing the Unknown

In the shadows, courage stirs,
A dance of whispers, soft as fur.
With every step, we feel the breeze,
Inviting us to bend our knees.

Fear melts like frost in warming light,
As dawn unveils the velvet night.
Through uncertainty, we find our grace,
In tender hugs of time and space.

Every heartbeat, a chance to learn,
In the fire, our spirits churn.
With open arms, we welcome fate,
In the unknown, we create.

Each fork in the road holds a story,
Inviting us to seek our glory.
As paths diverge, we stand as one,
Embracing all that's yet undone.

With courage strong, we step outside,
Into the waves, an ebbing tide.
In this plunge, we find our home,
As flawed and beautiful, we roam.

The Path Less Traveled

In the woods where shadows play,
Footprints linger, lead the way.
Whispers of the trees abound,
Lost and found without a sound.

A fork appears, one way is bright,
The other cloaked in gentle night.
With every step, a choice unfolds,
The stories of the brave and bold.

Clouds drift softly in the air,
Life supplies its trials rare.
Embrace the twists, the bends we find,
The journey shapes the heart and mind.

Paths converge, yet diverge too,
Each one painted in a hue.
Though uncertain where they lead,
Courage sown is hope's own seed.

In stillness, answers echo clear,
Every choice conceived without fear.
The path less traveled, roads unseen,
Leads us to where we've never been.

Cerulean Skies of Change

Above, a canvas drapes so wide,
Painting dreams where hopes abide.
Cerulean strokes blend and weave,
A tapestry for those who believe.

Clouds grow heavy, change in sight,
Thunder speaks through rolling light.
Nature's symphony, a call to hear,
In every drop, the world is clear.

The winds whisper of what's to come,
Sowing seeds, the heart beats drum.
With every gust, fresh tales arise,
Through vibrant hues and darkened skies.

We gather strength from vibrant dawns,
Through the trials, the spirit dawns.
Embrace the storms, let courage reign,
For beauty lies in every change.

Cerulean skies, a breath anew,
Painting life in every hue.
From ash, we rise, renew our gaze,
Through shifting skies, we find our ways.

Pioneering New Vistas

Mountains high call out to me,
Wilderness wide, wild and free.
A spirit bold with heart ablaze,
Seeks horizons lost in haze.

New vistas dawn where shadows fall,
With every step, I heed the call.
Exploring paths unseen before,
Adventure waits beyond the door.

The sun breaks forth with golden light,
Illuminating endless flight.
Each moment whispers tales untold,
Amidst the warmth, the brave and bold.

I forge ahead with open eyes,
With every challenge, I rise.
Pioneering through thorny brambles,
With a heart that never gambles.

A map drawn from the heart's deep core,
The world revealed, I yearn for more.
Together we explore and roam,
In every vista, we find home.

Cascading Thoughts of What Could Be

In quiet moments, thoughts cascade,
Whispers of dreams that never fade.
Notes of longing fill the air,
A symphony of hope laid bare.

What lies beyond this tethered view?
Every wish, a step anew.
Imagining worlds that swell with light,
As shadows dance through day and night.

Each thought a drop in a stream of gold,
Stories of futures yet untold.
Cascading visions take their flight,
With boundless passion, hearts ignite.

What could be and what shall we see?
The heart, a compass, guides the free.
Through winding paths, we take the leap,
In dreams' embrace, we dive so deep.

Cascading through the unknown air,
Letting go of every care.
In these thoughts, we find our way,
To brighter paths, a new array.

The Lighthouse of Innovation

In the storm, a light shines bright,
Guiding dreams through the night.
Waves crash, ideas take flight,
A beacon's glow, a future in sight.

Voices echo in the air,
Inventions born from care.
A spark ignites, visions dare,
Collaboration, beyond compare.

Shadows retreat, clarity reigns,
In each challenge, wisdom gains.
Through the fog, the mind's domains,
Innovation's pulse, it entertains.

Crafting tales of what's to be,
Boundless as the endless sea.
With each wave, the heart feels free,
In the lighthouse, we find our key.

Together we will chart the course,
Creativity, our driving force.
In this haven, we'll source
The light that leads us to endorse.

Gazing at Infinity

Stars twinkle in the night sky,
A cosmic dance, oh how they fly.
Whispers of the universe sigh,
As we ponder our reason why.

In this vastness, thoughts untold,
Stories of the brave and bold.
Every shimmering light behold,
In the infinite, we unfold.

Time stands still, moments pause,
In this wonder, we find cause.
Every question, every clause,
In eternity's silent applause.

The horizon stretches far and wide,
A journey taken side by side.
In the unknown, we'll abide,
With hopes that will not subside.

Casting dreams into the void,
With each wish, hearts enjoyed.
In the infinite, fears destroyed,
Gazing at infinity, overjoyed.

Flickers of the Unimagined

In shadows deep, a spark ignites,
Ideas dance like firefly lights.
Mysteries whisper through the nights,
Flickers born from daring sights.

In the quiet, thoughts take form,
Challenging the status norm.
Innovation find its warm,
Through each trial, a creative storm.

Visions bloom like springtime flowers,
In the depths of midnight hours.
Each flicker gives the heart its powers,
Unseen worlds with endless towers.

A tapestry of hopes we weave,
In the unseen, we believe.
With every breath, we retrieve,
Flickers that the mind conceive.

In the uncharted, we will roam,
Crafting dreams that call us home.
Flickers shining, we will comb,
Through the vastness, never alone.

The Promise of Dawn

Softly breaking, the morning light,
A canvas painted pure and bright.
Nightly fears take their flight,
In the glow, a new insight.

Whispers of hope in the breeze,
Morning dew drips from the trees.
Promises written, a heart that sees,
In each moment, the spirit frees.

From darkness rises a vibrant hue,
As the world awakens, born anew.
Each ray carries dreams that grew,
In the promise, we find our cue.

The horizon stretches, colors blend,
New beginnings on which we depend.
Embrace the day, let hearts ascend,
In this promise, love will mend.

So let us greet this sacred time,
With open hearts and thoughts sublime.
In the dawn, we find our rhyme,
Together, we'll reach our prime.

The Alchemy of Ideas

In the cauldron of thought, they brew,
Whispers of dreams rise anew.
Spark of a notion, a flicker aflame,
Transforming the dull into brilliant acclaim.

Gold from the shadows, truth to behold,
Ideas like stories, waiting to unfold.
With each gentle nudge, they dance and they sway,
Creating a world where imagination plays.

Moments of silence, the mind starts to churn,
From vision to vision, the wheels start to turn.
Fleeting reflections, a chase through the night,
In the alchemy of ideas, we find the light.

Hands intertwined, we shape and we mold,
Embracing the strange and the unfamiliar bold.
The magic ignites, and possibilities soar,
In the heart of the thinker, forever explore.

Each thought a treasure, vast and profound,
In the garden of wisdom, where answers abound.
With love and belief, we'll forge a new way,
In the alchemy of ideas, we find our stay.

Illuminating Hidden Paths

Beneath the surface, where shadows play,
Lie secret trails, lost in the fray.
A flicker of light, a guiding hand,
Leading the way to the promised land.

Through mist and fog, our spirits wander,
In silence we search, and we ponder.
With each step taken, the unknown revealed,
The heart of the journey, a truth unconcealed.

Whispers of wisdom, softly they call,
Encouraging souls who stumble and fall.
With courage ignited, we rise from the dark,
Guided by love, we ignite the spark.

Paths intertwined, no longer alone,
Together we tread, our spirits have grown.
Illuminating roads that once were obscured,
In the dance of the heart, we find what's pure.

With each revelation, a light we instill,
Paths once forgotten, now flourish at will.
Through valleys and mountains, together we stride,
Illuminating hidden paths with pride.

The Pursuit of the Unknowable

In the realm of questions, we delve and we seek,
Through layers of meaning, the curious peak.
Chasing the moments that slip through our grip,
In the pursuit of the unknowable, we take a trip.

Stars whisper secrets, ancient and wise,
Inviting our hearts to look beyond the skies.
With every inquiry, a door starts to creak,
Revealing the wonders that language can't speak.

The uncharted waters, where knowledge does flow,
Curiosity guides us, as we venture below.
In pursuit of the truths that elude even time,
We dance through the chaos, our spirits sublime.

With questions as anchors, we float on the sea,
Exploring the depths of what may never be.
In the silence of wonder, connection we find,
The pursuit of the unknowable, intertwined.

Each step taken bravely, a gift to the soul,
In the vastness of mystery, we uncover the whole.
With hearts wide open, in ever-expanding grace,
The pursuit of the unknowable, our destined place.

Horizons of Hope

As dawn breaks anew, with colors so bright,
Hope whispers softly, dispelling the night.
In the distance we see, a promise unfolds,
Horizons beckon, where courage upholds.

Through valleys of doubt, we wander and strive,
In the warmth of the sun, our dreams come alive.
With each step we take, new visions arise,
Filling our hearts with the light from the skies.

Beneath every struggle, a purpose is clear,
In the echoes of hardship, our spirits draw near.
Horizons of hope call, as we journey on,
Guided by stars, from dusk until dawn.

Hand in hand, through the storms that we face,
We'll cultivate strength, in this sacred space.
With open hearts, and resilience our guide,
Horizons of hope stretch, far and wide.

In the tapestry woven with threads of our dreams,
Hope shines brilliantly, illuminating seams.
As we reach for the future, together we cope,
In the arms of tomorrow, we nurture our hope.

Horizon's Embrace

The sun dips low, a gentle kiss,
Waves whisper secrets, a fleeting bliss.
Colors blend in twilight's view,
Nature's canvas, brushed anew.

Birds take flight, a dance in the air,
Chasing shadows without a care.
Stars emerge in the dusky light,
Guiding hearts into the night.

A bond with earth and sky is made,
In quiet moments, fears do fade.
Embrace the peace, let spirits soar,
Boundless horizons, forevermore.

Time flows like a river's song,
In this embrace, we all belong.
With every breath, we find our place,
In the vastness of time and space.

Dreamweavers Ahead

In the dawn of dreams, shadows fade,
Whispers of hope in twilight laid.
Casting visions like stars above,
Weaving tales of light and love.

Echoes of laughter fill the air,
Each thread spun with delicate care.
Creating worlds we yearn to embrace,
Dreamweavers dance in a sacred space.

The path unfolds with colors bright,
Guided by passion, we chase the light.
Every heartbeat sings a new refrain,
In the tapestry of joy and pain.

Through valleys deep and mountains high,
We soar on wings that never die.
For every dream is a story told,
A journey through the brave and bold.

In this weaving, we find our thread,
With every heartbeat, courage spread.
So let us walk where dreams align,
And in our hearts, let visions shine.

Unfolding the Future

Petals bloom, the dawn awakes,
Promises whisper in gentle shakes.
Time unfurls with each soft sigh,
In the quiet, hopes learn to fly.

Paths unknown stretch far and wide,
A journey pushed by dreams inside.
With every step, a chance to grow,
In folds of fate, the seeds we sow.

Clouds gather, skies might weep,
Yet in our hearts, we dare to leap.
With open hands and minds set free,
We mold the future, you and me.

Embrace the change, let worries cease,
In every ending, find new peace.
For the dawn comes after the night,
And in the shadows, shines the light.

So let us weave the threads of fate,
In every moment, learn, create.
Together we'll face the vast unknown,
In every heartbeat, love has grown.

Illuminated Pathways

A lantern glows, a guiding flame,
Casting shadows that call our name.
Step by step, we tread the night,
With every heartbeat, find the light.

Trees stand tall, their branches sway,
Whispering secrets along the way.
Paths diverge in quiet grace,
Adventure beckons, we embrace.

Stars above, a map so clear,
Leading wanderers who persevere.
In shadows cast, the truth reveals,
A journey driven by what we feel.

Hand in hand, we forge ahead,
With every story gently said.
Illuminated by dreams we share,
Creating moments, rich and rare.

For every step, a memory made,
In this life's dance, we won't evade.
So light the way, let hearts ignite,
In illuminated pathways, we find our might.

Worlds Beyond the Present

In shadows deep, we search for light,
Beyond the veil, in endless night.
Where echoes of the past still play,
And dreams of future find their way.

The stars above, they call our name,
In cosmic dance, we are the same.
With every breath, a new door blends,
To realms where time and space transcends.

Through whispered winds, our spirits soar,
To lands where minds can roam and explore.
In silence, truth begins to gleam,
Awakening within, a vibrant dream.

Each moment held, a precious gift,
In worlds unknown, our souls can drift.
The tapestry of fate we weave,
In lands where we can truly believe.

Embrace the thoughts that brightly spark,
As we ignite the endless dark.
For in our hearts, the maps reside,
To worlds beyond, where hope abides.

Journey into Unseen Realities

With every step, we leave the known,
A path unwritten, seeds are sown.
In whispers soft, the secrets glean,
Of what lies in the space between.

The rivers flow with thoughts unvoiced,
In shadows where our minds rejoice.
Together we traverse the fields,
Where every dream and truth reveals.

A realm of visions, vast and bright,
We wander through the endless night.
With eager hearts and open eyes,
We'll chase the sparks that light the skies.

The mountains echo with our calls,
In unseen worlds, the silence falls.
Each moment taken, precious and rare,
In journeys bold, we breathe the air.

Through unseen tracks, our spirits race,
In resonances of time and space.
With every word a step we take,
Towards realities we long to make.

The Craft of Imagination

In quiet hours, the mind takes flight,
Where dreams are spun from threads of light.
The canvas blank, the vision clear,
In realms of thought, we have no fear.

With brush of hope, we paint the skies,
In colors bright, our spirits rise.
Each stroke a world, each thought a chance,
Where fantasies and wonders dance.

We craft the tales that shape our days,
In whispered lines and wondrous ways.
Through labyrinths of thought we sail,
In every heart, a hidden trail.

The stories bloom like stars at night,
Illuminating paths of might.
In vivid hues, our dreams unfold,
In every heart, a tale retold.

The craft of dreams, a noble art,
Where every vision plays its part.
With open minds and daring souls,
We shape the world, we reach our goals.

Celestial Blueprints

Beneath the stars, a plan is laid,
In cosmic sketches, essences spade.
The moonlight dances on the ground,
In every shadow, truths are found.

Galaxies whisper of our past,
In nebulae, the shadows cast.
Blueprints drawn in stardust flow,
As we explore what we don't know.

Each comet's flight, a mapped design,
In tangled threads, our lives align.
The universe, a wondrous scheme,
Awakens within our deepest dream.

In every heartbeat, rhythms blend,
Connecting us, a timeless friend.
Through cosmic paths, we navigate,
In celestial blueprints, we create.

With open hearts, we chart the skies,
In awe of wonders, we arise.
Each star a guide, each night a chance,
To find our truth in cosmic dance.

Kaleidoscope of Ideas

Colors twist and turn with grace,
Thoughts collide in a warm embrace.
Shapes of dreams begin to bloom,
In a dance that fills the room.

Every vision, a story told,
In sparkling hues, both bold and old.
The world spins bright, a vibrant dance,
Inviting us to take a chance.

With every turn, a new surprise,
Awakening wonder in our eyes.
Fragments shimmer, then unite,
Creating beauty in the light.

Ideas flow like rivers deep,
In this tapestry, we leap.
With open minds, we share and grow,
In this kaleidoscope, we glow.

A Symphony of Futures

Notes of hope fill the air,
A melody beyond compare.
Chords of dreams ring out so clear,
Inviting us to draw them near.

Timeless echoes, soft and sweet,
Embrace our hearts, our souls repeat.
Every sound a path to trace,
In this world of endless space.

Rhythms pulse, entwined with fate,
Each step taken opens a gate.
In the harmony of our quest,
We chase horizons, never rest.

Tuning visions in the night,
Together we compose the light.
In every heartbeat, futures sing,
A symphony, all life can bring.

In the Realm of What-Ifs

Waves of thought drift through the air,
Imagination sows, seeds of care.
Each query holds a spark of chance,
Inviting us to dream and dance.

In whispers soft, possibilities sway,
Carving paths that lead away.
The what-ifs build a bridge to dream,
Transforming fantasies into gleam.

Through shadows cast, new visions grow,
In the realm where ideas flow.
We ponder wonders yet to be,
In a world where we all dream free.

With open hearts, we take the leap,
Into the depths of thoughts we keep.
In this place, the future bends,
And every question sparks, transcends.

Threads of Imagination

Spools of color line the shelves,
Waiting for us to weave ourselves.
Each thread a story, bright and bold,
Connecting dreams yet to unfold.

In tapestry of endless night,
Patterns emerge, a dazzling sight.
Every twist, a journey new,
In the fabric of all we pursue.

Moments stitched in time and space,
Creating warmth, a shared embrace.
The loom of life spins fast and wide,
In this creation, we reside.

With nimble fingers, we design,
In every thread, our hopes align.
Through imagination's hands, we find,
The beauty woven, intertwined.

Whispers of Unseen Paths

In the silence where shadows entwine,
Footsteps echo, a rhythm divine.
Leaves murmur secrets, wind softly sighs,
Guiding us onward, where mystery lies.

Stars are the lanterns, glowing so bright,
Illuminating dreams in the depth of night.
Every twist leads to a story untold,
A map of the heart, in colors bold.

Wisdom flows gently, like rivers in spring,
Whispers of fate in the songs they sing.
Paths may obscure, yet hope will remain,
In the journey of life, embrace the refrain.

Time ticks softly, a clockwork of grace,
Every moment a step towards our place.
Through valleys and peaks, the spirit shall soar,
Awakening wonders we never knew before.

So let every whisper guide us anew,
In the unseen paths, find the courage to pursue.
Together in silence, we will unfold,
The stories of us, yet to be told.

Gazing Through the Kaleidoscope

Colors collide in a vibrant swirl,
Patterns that dance, twist, and unfurl.
A glimpse of the world through fragmented glass,
Moments in time, fleeting and fast.

Reflections of laughter, echoes of tears,
A prism of memories across the years.
In every shift, new stories arise,
Revealing the truth behind myriad lies.

Each turn of the lens paints a tale,
In shades of the heart where shadows prevail.
Whispers of wonder, dreams intertwined,
In the kaleidoscope's grasp, beauty we find.

Stillness holds magic, inviting the gaze,
Life's intricate dance in a shimmering haze.
Through the lens of love, we see what we seek,
Moments of joy in the vibrant mystique.

So gaze and behold, the world spins around,
In every reflection, a new truth is found.
With a heart wide open, embrace every phase,
In the kaleidoscope's light, forever amaze.

Seeds of Tomorrow's Wonders

In the soil of dreams, we plant our seeds,
Nurtured by hope, and watered by needs.
Each tiny sprout, a promise to grow,
In the garden of time, love tends the flow.

Seasons will change, yet the roots run deep,
Through winters of doubt, we learn how to keep.
Sunshine and rain, a dance of the skies,
Fostering futures where beauty will rise.

With patience we tend, through trials we face,
The bounty of life, a tender embrace.
From whispers of courage, blossoms will thrive,
In the seeds of tomorrow, our dreams come alive.

In the tapestry woven, each thread has its place,
A symphony played in nature's own grace.
Together we nurture, together we stand,
Creating a world by our own loving hand.

So plant your ideas in the gardens of hope,
Watch them take root, learn the art of cope.
For every small seed holds untold power,
In the heart of the earth, we bloom as a flower.

The Light Beyond the Tunnel

In shadows we wander, seeking the glimmer,
A flicker of hope, a light that won't dimmer.
Through passages dark, where fears intertwine,
The promise of dawn in the depths we find.

Step by step forward, the heart beats a tune,
Guided by whispers of sun and of moon.
Each inhale of courage, each exhale of pain,
We rise through the struggles, like spring after rain.

With every deep breath, we kindle the spark,
Illuminating pathways once cloaked in the dark.
For the journey is long, yet the end we can see,
A horizon of light where our spirits fly free.

As shadows recede, and the dawn breaks anew,
Hope paints the canvas in vibrant hues.
Together we'll rise, with the sun on our face,
In the light beyond tunnels, we find our true place.

So trust in the journey, embrace every mile,
For even in darkness, you'll find room to smile.
The light will lead on, through the valleys and bends,
In the story of life, where beginnings transcend.

Sculpting Tomorrow's Landscape

With every thought, we shape the clay,
Ideas swirling, bright as day.
Hands of vision, guided intent,
Crafting futures, wherever we went.

Roots of knowledge, deep and wide,
Growing dreams, with hope as our guide.
The skyline shifts, a canvas vast,
We sketch the future, break from the past.

Nature whispers in a gentle breeze,
Harmony blooms among the trees.
Building bridges, connecting souls,
In this landscape, we pay our tolls.

Molding fears into stones of strength,
With every step, we go the length.
Sculpting futures, bold and bright,
For the dawn of a new light.

Each grain of sand, a world unknown,
As we create, we've truly grown.
With hands united, we'll share the load,
Sculpting tomorrow, on this bright road.

Wings of Innovation

Soaring high on thought's own wing,
A symphony of change we sing.
Ideas birthed in minds so bold,
A future rich, with stories told.

Bright sparks ignite the darkest night,
With every breakthrough, hearts take flight.
Inventive minds, a restless sea,
In waves of change, we feel so free.

Challenges faced with courage grand,
Together we rise, hand in hand.
Unyielding spirit, fierce and bright,
With every dream, we own the night.

Harnessing passion, burning high,
Against the odds, we reach the sky.
Wings of progress, spread so wide,
In innovation, we take pride.

A journey crafted through each trial,
With every step, we walk a mile.
Through valleys low, and mountains steep,
In innovation's embrace, we leap.

Lanterns of Hopeful Minds

Flickering lights in the darkened night,
Lanterns of hope, guiding our sight.
Each glow a promise, warm and clear,
Illuminating paths that draw us near.

Voices united, echoing bright,
In harmony, we find our light.
Through shadows thick, we weave and bind,
Drawing strength from a hopeful mind.

A tapestry woven, stories unfold,
In every thread, a dream to hold.
With gentle hands, we mend the seams,
Giving life to all our dreams.

In the quiet moments, we will see,
The power in you, the power in me.
Lanterns flicker, but never fade,
Together, our legacy is laid.

With every step, a light we share,
Bound by the love in the open air.
Hope's gentle glow, forever shines,
In the hearts of all hopeful minds.

Gazing into New Dimensions

Open your eyes to worlds anew,
Dimensions layered, shades of blue.
A journey deep, the heart's desire,
In every glance, ignites the fire.

Shifting perspectives, a wondrous sight,
In every shadow, there's a light.
Through the portal of the mind,
A universe of color, we will find.

Exploring depths, both vast and wide,
In every corner, dreams reside.
Unlock the doors, embrace the chance,
In unfamiliar lands, we can dance.

Echoes of wisdom softly call,
In every rise, in every fall.
Gazing forward, we won't lose sight,
As new dimensions claim the night.

With each new thought, a pathway clear,
In the unknown, we shed our fear.
Together, let's break through the haze,
Gazing forward, into the blaze.

The Tapestry of Tomorrow's Dreams

In whispers soft, dreams weave their thread,
Beneath the stars, where wishes tread.
Each stitch a hope, a vision clear,
A tapestry where hearts draw near.

Through valleys wide, horizons gleam,
Awakening the slumbering dream.
Patterns blend in vibrant hues,
Creating paths that one can choose.

With every turn, a story grows,
In the silence, the heartbeat flows.
The fabric shifts, as futures call,
Embracing all, both great and small.

Threads of courage, strands of light,
Guide the way through darkest night.
Entwined in hope, we find our place,
In this rich, embracing space.

A weaving bright, with love imbued,
Tomorrow's dreams, a life renewed.

The Light of Possibility

A flicker stirs in twilight's glow,
The dawn awakes, the shadows slow.
In every heart, a spark ignites,
Illuminating endless heights.

With open arms, the world expands,
Embracing dreams that fate commands.
Each moment holds a chance to see,
The light that dwells, so wild and free.

Through tangled paths, we find our way,
In every choice, a brighter day.
A beacon shines in darkest fear,
A call to rise, to persevere.

The dawn unfolds, horizons blend,
In the space where hope transcends.
With every step, the heart can find,
The light of truth that once seemed blind.

Each thought a spark, each word a flame,
As possibility calls our name.

Shaping the Unseen

In quiet whispers, shadows dance,
Life breathes softly, given a chance.
We sculpt the dreams that ebb and flow,
Forging paths where hearts might go.

With hands of vision, we carve out space,
Creating forms that time can't trace.
In every gesture, a story lies,
Beneath the surface, wisdom cries.

Through intricate layers, we seek to find,
The beauty that lies intertwined.
Each unseen force begins to gleam,
Manifesting the power of dream.

Each thought a brush, each breath a tool,
Shaping essence, breaking the rule.
In this dance of the great unknown,
We find the seeds of what we've sown.

Through silent echoes, we build and break,
Crafting the world, for our own sake.

Dreamweaver's Map

Beneath the stars, a map unfolds,
Of whispered dreams and tales retold.
Guided by visions of what may be,
Through lands of wonder, wild and free.

With every line, a journey starts,
Tracing the rhythms of beating hearts.
In vibrant colors, paths diverge,
A symphony of dreams emerge.

Each twist and turn, a dance of fate,
Where courage blooms, and fears abate.
In ink of hope, we mark the way,
Navigating the light of day.

The dreamweaver's craft, a tale aligned,
With whispers of lost souls entwined.
From dusk to dawn, the journey calls,
Through hidden gates, past ancient walls.

With open eyes, the map we chart,
Unfolding dreams that seek the heart.

Guardians of Tomorrow's Wisdom

In the quiet of the night, we stand,
Guardians of knowledge, hand in hand.
Through whispered tales of ages past,
We forge a future, firm and vast.

With eyes like stars, we seek the light,
Embracing shadows, banishing fright.
Each lesson learned, a bridge we build,
To shape a world, our dreams fulfilled.

With gentle hearts, we guide the youth,
Nurturing seeds of hope and truth.
In every question, we find the key,
Unlocking doors to what can be.

Through trials faced, we find our ground,
In the echoes of wisdom, we're forever bound.
Together we rise, with spirits bright,
For tomorrow's wisdom, we stand and fight.

In the tapestry of life, we weave,
Stories of vision, dreams to believe.
With each new dawn, our purpose clear,
Guardians of tomorrow, we hold dear.

Dreams in Motion

In the realm where visions soar,
Dreams in motion, we explore.
With every step, our hearts ignite,
Painting colors in the night.

Whispers of hope in the gentle breeze,
Carry our wishes, put our minds at ease.
Through valleys low and mountains high,
We chase the stars, we learn to fly.

In every heartbeat, a story lies,
An echo of laughter, a thousand sighs.
Through trials faced, we hold on tight,
For in our dreams, we find the light.

Moments fleeting, like grains of sand,
As we dance through life, hand in hand.
With every swirl, our spirit glows,
In dreams in motion, our essence flows.

So let us run, let us embrace,
The wild journey, the endless race.
For in the chase, we truly find,
The dreams in motion that free the mind.

Eureka Moments in Time

In the stillness, ideas spark,
Eureka moments in the dark.
From silent whispers, genius born,
A future forged, a path is worn.

Through tangled thoughts, we weave a thread,
Connecting dots of what we've said.
With open hearts and eager minds,
In every search, a treasure finds.

From chaos rose, a flash of truth,
Illuminating the quest for proof.
Within that instant, worlds collide,
And in the wonder, we take pride.

With every breakthrough, we rise anew,
Building the bridges of what is true.
The sparks of brilliance, we hold dear,
Eureka moments shining clear.

So gather 'round, embrace the chance,
To seek the magic in life's dance.
In every thought, a story chimes,
Celebrating eureka moments in time.

The Echoing Future

In the silence, we hear the call,
The echoing future, over all.
With whispers past, the tales align,
A symphony of dreams divine.

Each step forward, a path we trace,
Bringing hope to every place.
With every voice, a story sung,
From ancient earth to the young.

As time unfolds, we shape the way,
Casting shadows on yesterday.
With hands united, we build and strive,
In the echoing future, we come alive.

For every heart has dreams to share,
With compassion woven into the air.
Together we rise, as one we stand,
In the echoing future, hand in hand.

So let us listen, let us learn,
For in our hearts, the fires burn.
In every echo, a promise lies,
Guiding the future, where hope flies.

Merging Minds

Two thoughts collide in silent night,
Shared whispers echo, taking flight.
In the stillness, dreams align,
Creating worlds where stars entwine.

A glance exchanged, ideas flow,
Crafting visions, hearts aglow.
Boundless spaces, thoughts expand,
Together crafting, hand in hand.

In this realm, the magic brews,
Infinite paths, countless clues.
One mind grows, another soars,
Deep connections unlocks doors.

With every laugh, a spark ignites,
Fueling the passion that excites.
In unity, we rise and shine,
Interwoven, your heart in mine.

Through shadows cast, we'll find our way,
Braving storms, come what may.
Together forging brighter days,
In merging minds, love conquers gray.

In the Labyrinth of Possibilities

A maze of dreams, twists and bends,
Where every turn, a new path sends.
Fingers trace the walls of fate,
Seeking light that can't be late.

Whispers linger in the air,
Echoes of hope, beyond despair.
Winding roads keep hearts alive,
In this space, we strive and thrive.

Questions linger, answers hide,
In shadows where secrets bide.
A choice awaits, the heart must dare,
Navigating through a silent prayer.

The journey weaves in colors bright,
Each moment, a chance to ignite.
Paths converge then drift apart,
In this labyrinth, we find our heart.

With every exit, a new begin,
A chance to face the world within.
Through tangled routes, we come to see,
In every choice, we're truly free.

A Dance with Tomorrow

Beneath the stars, we start our dance,
In rhythms that defy mere chance.
Every heartbeat hints at fate,
In twilight's grip, we innovate.

Steps unfolding, futures bright,
Swirling dreams in endless night.
The dawn whispers, a silent tune,
As we waltz toward the coming boon.

In every sway, a promise lives,
In mutual trust, our spirit gives.
With every turn, we chance the fall,
In this embrace, we conquer all.

Tomorrow's light on our backs glows,
Guiding us where the river flows.
Hand in hand, we'll forge our way,
In this dance, come what may.

As shadows fade, the day breaks near,
The magic lingers, forever clear.
In moments shared, life's beauty shows,
In a dance with tomorrow, love grows.

Chronicles of the Untamed Mind

In wild thoughts, the stories bloom,
A tapestry spun in shadowed room.
Ink spills freely, ideas break,
A journey twists with every take.

Through tangled roots of yesteryears,
Forgotten dreams and uncried tears.
Each page turned, a voice demands,
To rise up strong, to take bold stands.

In chaos wrapped, beauty lies,
The untamed spark beneath the skies.
With every word, the soul takes flight,
In whispered tales, we seek the light.

Adventures penned in hearts ablaze,
With every sentence, we'll amaze.
The chronicle we write today,
Is stitched with hopes that never fray.

Through trials faced, the mind remains,
A vessel filled with joys and pains.
In the vastness of the human find,
We celebrate the untamed mind.

Lighthouses in the Fog

Amidst the mist, they stand so tall,
Guiding the lost through night's deep call.
With beams of hope, they pierce the gloom,
A shimmer of light in an uncertain room.

Waves crash against their weathered stone,
In silence they watch, never alone.
With every blink, they whisper dreams,
Of shores unseen and moonlit beams.

The fog rolls in, a blanket wide,
Yet still they shine, a faithful guide.
With every storm, their courage grows,
A steady heart that forever glows.

They tell of sailors who've come and gone,
Of journeys taken at the break of dawn.
Through troubled seas and darkened skies,
They shine the truth where hope still lies.

In every flicker, a tale unfolds,
Of love and loss that the ocean holds.
Each lighthouse stands, a sentinel bright,
In the vast expanse of the endless night.

Chasing Shadows of Tomorrow

In the twilight, shadows dance and play,
We chase the dreams that slip away.
Footsteps echo on paths unknown,
A gentle breeze, a whispered tone.

With every step, we yearn for light,
To guide us through the darkest night.
With open hearts, we seek and find,
The pieces of a future intertwined.

As stars begin to grace the sky,
We hold our hopes, never shy.
In every shadow, a story lies,
Of laughter shared and endless ties.

Through winding roads and twists of fate,
We forge ahead, it's never too late.
With courage sparked, we break the dawn,
Chasing shadows till the light is drawn.

In every moment, we live and dream,
With eyes wide open to the gleam.
Together we rise, against the sorrow,
With faith alive in the bright tomorrow.

Mapping the Stars

Upon the canvas of the night,
Stars are drawn, a wondrous sight.
Each constellation tells a tale,
Of ancient dreams that still prevail.

With whispers soft, the cosmos calls,
In silent awe, our spirit falls.
We chart the paths of light and dark,
In endless journeys, we leave our mark.

Galaxies swirl in a cosmic dance,
Gravity pulls us in a trance.
Each twinkling light, a beacon bright,
Guides lost souls through the endless night.

In darkness deep, we find our way,
With starlit maps to guide our play.
Through every point, a history flows,
Of lost loves and the heart's throes.

As we gaze up, our hearts ignite,
In dreams that soar, we take flight.
To map the stars, a noble quest,
In cosmic wonder, we find our rest.

Celestial Threads of Imagination

In the loom of night, dreams are spun,
Celestial threads, our journey begun.
With colors bright, we weave our fate,
In the tapestry where visions await.

Each thought a stitch, each wish a tie,
Binding the earth to the endless sky.
With every breath, we craft our tale,
A dance of visions that will not stale.

Through realms unknown, our spirits soar,
On wings of wonder, we explore.
In nebula's glow, our hopes reside,
A universe vast, our dreams the guide.

In every thread, a spark of light,
Illuminates worlds hidden from sight.
With hands outstretched, we seek and find,
The beauty of hearts, intricately intertwined.

As stars align, we take our stand,
In this cosmic weave, we hold our hands.
For in imagination's gentle thread,
We find our dreams and the paths ahead.

Seeds of Tomorrow's Light

In the soil of dreams we sow,
Tiny hopes begin to grow.
With each raindrop, whispers sing,
Of the joys that future brings.

Sunshine kisses leaves so sweet,
Nourished roots embrace the heat.
Through the dark and through the grey,
These small seeds will find their way.

Time will weave its gentle thread,
Each blossom from where we've tread.
Hands once empty, now hold tight,
To the seeds of tomorrow's light.

Buds unfurl with colors bold,
Stories waiting to be told.
In the garden, life's delight,
Sprouts the dreams that take their flight.

Let the winds of change then guide,
Hearts that carry hope inside.
With each step, we plant anew,
Seeds of light with morning dew.

Chasing Shadows of Innovation

In the twilight of the mind,
New creations wait to find.
Ideas swirl in dusky air,
Chasing shadows everywhere.

Bright reflections dance and play,
In the depths of night and day.
Through the paths of thought we roam,
Building dreams to call our home.

Voices whisper in the dark,
Lighting up a glowing spark.
In the chaos, find the clue,
Chasing shadows to break through.

Inventive spirits rise and shine,
Crafting visions so divine.
With each moment, futures gleam,
Chasing shadows of our dream.

In the heart of bold desire,
Lies the fuel, the inner fire.
To create, to innovate,
Chasing shadows, shaping fate.

Mapping the Unseen

In the quiet space we dwell,
Lies a story yet to tell.
Hidden realms with paths unknown,
Map the places we have grown.

Between the lines of what is real,
Whispers of the soul reveal.
Through the fog, let visions guide,
Mapping truths that long abide.

Every heartbeat leaves a mark,
Tracing journeys in the dark.
With a compass, brave and bold,
Charting dreams that will unfold.

In the silence, secrets wake,
Through the shadows, paths we take.
Though the world may hide from view,
Mapping what we know is true.

Underneath the surface lies,
All the wonders shaped in skies.
With each step, horizons gleam,
Mapping the unseen we dream.

Beyond the Veil of Possibility

In the mist of what could be,
Lies a world for us to see.
Dancing lightly on the edge,
Beyond the veil, we make a pledge.

With our hearts and minds in sync,
We will rise, we will not sink.
In the spaces, futures play,
Beyond the veil, we find our way.

Every challenge becomes a key,
Unlocking doors to set us free.
In the twilight, hopes awake,
Beyond the veil, new paths we take.

Let imagination soar so high,
Reaching out to touch the sky.
In the whispers of the night,
Beyond the veil, we find our light.

With each breath, embrace the dream,
Life's a canvas, let us scheme.
In the end, we shall fulfill,
Beyond the veil, with strength and will.

Revelations of the Unimagined

In shadows where dreams reside,
Whispers of fate gently collide.
Visions shatter the silent night,
Awakening hopes in the pale light.

The stars unveil their hidden tales,
Each a ship with flapping sails.
Boundless skies invite the brave,
To seek the depths of the unknown wave.

Colors merge where silence stirs,
Awakening life as magic purrs.
Unfold the fabric of time anew,
Crafting paths where none once flew.

From endless voids, horizons bloom,
Filling hearts with sweet perfume.
In every heartbeat, secrets whirl,
Unimagined worlds begin to unfurl.

So listen close, for they will share,
The whispered truths that hang in air.
Embrace the light that bends and sways,
Revel in the unimagined ways.

The Canvas of Tomorrow

With brushes dipped in dreams of gold,
We paint the future, bold and untold.
A canvas stretched, a pure expanse,
Each stroke a spark, each line a dance.

Colors clash, yet harmonize,
Underneath the vast, bright skies.
Shades of hope, and whispers deep,
In the art of life, our souls we keep.

Imagination's brush, a steady hand,
Carving visions across the land.
Echoes of laughter fill the air,
As dreams take form, beyond compare.

Tomorrow waits in vibrant hues,
In every heart, a spark renews.
The canvas grows with each new day,
Painting pathways as we sway.

From thrill of dusk to dawn's bright light,
We craft our fate with pure delight.
In every splash, a story flows,
On the canvas of tomorrow, hope glows.

Embracing the Future's Pulse

In every heartbeat, time's embrace,
A rhythm of change sets the pace.
With open arms, we find our way,
Embracing dreams that dance and sway.

Moments fade, yet feelings stay,
Guiding us through the fray.
A pulse of promise, bright and bold,
In silent whispers, futures unfold.

Stars align, the cosmos sings,
Carving paths from wondrous things.
Hope ignites with every breath,
Defying limits, conquering death.

The future glimmers just ahead,
Where vibrant visions brightly spread.
Through trials faced, we rise, we soar,
In every pulse, we seek for more.

So let us dance to life's sweet tune,
Beneath the gaze of the silver moon.
With courage firm and hearts ablaze,
We embrace the future's endless ways.

Kindle the Dawn

As night retreats and shadows yield,
A new horizon is revealed.
The sun ascends, ignites the sky,
Kindling hope as moments fly.

Soft whispers of the dawn ignite,
Fragile dreams take wing in flight.
Each ray a promise, bright and bold,
A story waiting to be told.

Golden beams on dew-kissed land,
Awakening life, the world at hand.
With gentle arms, we rise anew,
In every heartbeat, spirits flew.

Chasing light where shadows lay,
Every challenge shapes the day.
From darkness, strength begins to grow,
As dawn illuminates the glow.

So kindle the fire, let it blaze,
In every moment, find your ways.
Embrace the morning, fresh and bright,
Kindle the dawn, ignite your light.

Awakening the Infinite

In whispers low, the dawn unfolds,
A canvas fresh, with tales untold.
The sun ignites the waking skies,
Awakening dreams, where magic lies.

Through shadows deep, the light will creep,
Awakening souls from slumbered sleep.
With every breath, a chance to rise,
Embracing hope that never dies.

The heartbeats sound, a rhythm wild,
Awakening the dreamer's child.
In every spark, the cosmos sways,
Unraveling threads of endless ways.

As galaxies collide, we find our place,
Awakening us to the vast embrace.
Where stardust dances, destiny weaves,
In every moment, the universe believes.

So dare to leap into the unknown,
Awakening wonders yet to be grown.
With open arms, we stride ahead,
Towards the infinite, where we are led.

The Foresight Chronicles

In shadows cast by future's hand,
The Foresight Chronicles take their stand.
Through pages worn, the visions clear,
Unfolding paths that draw us near.

With every turn, a tale of fate,
The whispers guide, we contemplate.
Moments etched in time's embrace,
Unraveling dreams we dare to chase.

Eyes wide open, we seek the light,
In the chronicles, we find our might.
As time unwinds the threads we weave,
In foresight's glow, we must believe.

For every choice, a world anew,
In the chronicles, possibilities brew.
With every heartbeat, we craft our story,
In the realm of foresight, we find our glory.

So let us write with bold intent,
The Foresight Chronicles, our lives' lament.
In pages turned, our voices soar,
Together we dream, forevermore.

Insights from Distant Shores

Across the waves, a whisper flows,
Insights gathered from distant shores.
In every tide, a lesson learned,
With every heartbeat, insights churned.

The salt of life, it stings and heals,
In distant lands, the heart reveals.
Through eyes that wander, we find our song,
In every tale, where we belong.

The winds carry stories from afar,
Guiding us under the same bright star.
With every step on foreign ground,
In distant shores, our truths are found.

Embrace the journey, the unknown awaits,
Insights waiting to reconfigure fates.
Through unity in diversity, we rise,
Learning the wisdom that never dies.

So sail toward horizons yet unseen,
Insights from shores where we've never been.
In every wave, a chance to grow,
Through distant whispers, our spirits flow.

Sculptors of Tomorrow

With hands of clay, we mold the dreams,
Sculptors of Tomorrow, or so it seems.
In every touch, the future's cast,
Creating beauty from shadows past.

The chisel strikes with purpose clear,
Sculptors of Tomorrow, we persevere.
In visions bold, our hopes take flight,
Crafting a world from the depths of night.

Through trials faced and battles won,
Sculptors of Tomorrow, our work's begun.
With every curve, our stories flow,
Carving pathways where love will grow.

United we stand as artisans brave,
Sculptors of Tomorrow, the paths we pave.
In every heart, the vision ignites,
A canvas bright, where future unites.

So let us create with passion and fire,
Sculptors of Tomorrow, we shall inspire.
In every heartbeat, our values blend,
Together we shape what never ends.

The Horizon Calls

A whisper dances in the breeze,
Beyond the mountains, where sun meets trees.
Adventures await, just out of sight,
The horizon calls, igniting our flight.

With every step, the world expands,
New paths unfold like shifting sands.
The sky is vast, the dreams are bright,
We chase the dawn, embracing the light.

The echoes of hope, they softly sing,
In every heart, a spark takes wing.
Together we'll wander, together we'll roam,
In the arms of the unknown, we find our home.

Stars guide the way on this journey long,
In the silence, we hear the song.
With courage as our map and guide,
We venture forth, where dreams reside.

Each moment a canvas, painted anew,
A masterpiece formed in colors and hue.
The horizon beckons, bold and true,
In the sea of life, we are the crew.

Threads of Infinite Potential

In the fabric of life, threads intertwine,
Each story and dream, uniquely divine.
With every connection, a pattern is sewn,
Infinite potential in seeds we have grown.

Whispers of wisdom in moments we share,
The strength of our bond, a treasure so rare.
In the loom of time, we weave our fate,
Through laughter and tears, we cultivate.

Each thread tells a story, a journey begun,
In colors so vibrant, like rays of the sun.
Together we rise, through valleys and peaks,
In unity, our spirit speaks.

With courage and hope, we stitch the unknown,
In the tapestry of life, we're never alone.
For every connection, a spark ignites,
In threads of potential, our future ignites.

We laugh through the trials, we celebrate wins,
In the dance of our lives, the magic begins.
With hands intertwined, we venture ahead,
In the threads of tomorrow, our dreams are wed.

A Symphony of New Ideas

In the quiet of thought, melodies play,
A symphony of ideas, guiding the way.
Notes of inspiration, a vibrant song,
Together collectively, we all belong.

Innovation blooms in the minds of the bold,
Stories waiting to be shared and told.
In the harmony of voices, a vision takes flight,
Embracing the future, we chase the light.

Each idea a note, each thought a refrain,
In the orchestra of change, we flourish, not wane.
With courage and passion, we craft our score,
In the symphony of progress, we'll forever explore.

The rhythm of unity, we share and compose,
In the song of the ages, compassion grows.
Together we rise, our hearts synchronize,
In the explosion of sound, there's strength to arise.

With every new verse, we challenge the norms,
In the melody of life, creativity warms.
In this grand symphony, we find our place,
A celebration of ideas, where dreams embrace.

Navigating the Future's Seas

The horizon glimmers with promise and hope,
A canvas of dreams where we learn to cope.
With sails of ambition, we venture wide,
Navigating the future, our hearts as our guide.

Waves of the unknown crash against our boat,
Yet even in storms, we stay afloat.
Resilience and strength in every swell,
Through trials and triumphs, we weave our spell.

Together we journey, united we steer,
Through uncharted waters, we face every fear.
Stars above guide us along the way,
In the ocean of time, we seize the day.

With every new dawn, we chart our course,
In unity, we find our power and force.
With laughter and love as our constant drive,
In the vastness of life, we truly thrive.

As waves kiss the shore, horizons expand,
We embrace the future, hand in hand.
In the journey ahead, with courage, we meet,
Navigating the seas, our hearts skip a beat.

Envisioning New Worlds

In the hush of twilight glow,
We weave thoughts from stardust's flow.
Mountains rise from whispers deep,
Awake the dreams the cosmos keep.

Oceans dance with silver light,
Underneath the velvet night.
Crafting paths in cosmic skies,
Where imagination freely flies.

Lost in visions, bold and bright,
Every heartbeat fuels the flight.
New horizons call our name,
In the vastness, none the same.

From shadows born, the colors burst,
In every heart, a primal thirst.
To create, to change, to grow,
In endless realms, we bravely go.

Let the vision gently flow,
Through the valleys, over snow.
With every step, we redefine,
The worlds within, so vast, divine.

Tapestry of Electric Dreams

In the city's heartbeat, bright and bold,
Neon visions woven, mysteries told.
Threads of laughter, shimmers of light,
Painting dreams in the endless night.

Voices echo, collide and blend,
Each a story, around each bend.
Shadows dance in the vibrant glow,
In electric hues, imaginations flow.

The pulse of life, a spirited race,
Every moment, a tender embrace.
We chase the dawn, with open eyes,
In this tapestry, our spirit flies.

Fragments of dreams, alive and true,
In every heartbeat, me and you.
Woven together, we find our way,
In the electric fabric of the day.

So let us journey, hand in hand,
Through this landscape, vast and grand.
In the dance of shadows and beams,
We awaken in electric dreams.

Hues of a Bright Dawn

As the night gives way to day,
Golden rays chase shadows away.
Soft whispers brush the morning air,
In hues of hope, our spirits flare.

Crimson blushes greet the skies,
Buds awaken, and life replies.
The world is painted with gentle brush,
In the stillness, we feel the hush.

Birds ascend on wings of grace,
In every note, we find our place.
Nature sings in vibrant voice,
In every heartbeat, we rejoice.

The horizon glows, a canvas wide,
With every color, hearts open wide.
Together we rise, hand in hand,
Embracing the dawn, a promise grand.

With each sunrise, we redefine,
Paths we tread, the fates entwine.
In the palette of life, find your way,
In hues of a bright dawn, seize the day.

The Story Yet Unwritten

In the silence of unturned pages,
Lies the gift of countless stages.
With every breath, a tale yet told,
In every heart, a dream to hold.

Footprints lead to paths unknown,
In shadows cast, our strengths are shown.
With ink of courage, we begin,
The story waits where dreams have been.

Every moment, a whisper's charm,
In the unknown, we find our calm.
Let the pen dance, let it fly,
In the boundless sky, our dreams comply.

Characters bloom in vibrant hues,
In the narrative, we choose to lose.
With each chapter, we shape our fate,
In the story, we find our state.

A journey awaits, bold and bright,
With every word, we ignite the light.
For within us lies the strength to spin,
The tale of life, the story yet unwritten.

—